Communism and its Tactics by Sylvia Pankhurst
2011 Prism Key Press // www.prismkeypress.com

Communism and its Tactics
Sylvia Pankhurst

Contents

First Version

Part One

Workers Dreadnought VOL. VIII. No. 37 Saturday, November 26th, 1921

Under Communism all shall satisfy their material needs without stint or measure from the common storehouse, according to their desires. Everyone will be able to have what he or she desires in food, in clothing, books, music, education and travel facilities. The abundant production now possible, and which invention will constantly facilitate, will remove any need for rationing or limiting of consumption.

Every individual, relying on the great common production, will be secure from material want and anxiety.

There will be no class distinctions, since these arise from differences in material possessions, education and social status — all such distinctions will be swept away.

There will be neither rich nor poor. Money will no longer exist, and none will desire to hoard commodities not in use, since a fresh supply may be obtained at will. There will be no selling, because there will be no buyers, since everyone will be able to obtain everything at will, without payment.

The possession of private property, beyond that which is in actual personal use, will disappear.

There will be neither masters nor servants, all being in a position of economic equality — no individual will be able to become the employer of another.

All children will be educated up to adult age, and all

adults will be able to make free, unstinted use of all educational facilities in their abundant leisure.

Stealing, forgery, burglary, and all economic crimes will disappear, with all the objectionable apparatus for preventing, detecting and punishing them.

Prostitution will become extinct; it is a commercial transaction, dependent upon the economic need of the prostitute and the customer's power to pay.

Sexual union will no longer be based upon material conditions, but will be freely contracted on the basis of affection and mutual attraction.

The birth of children will cease to be prevented by reason of poverty.

Material anxiety being removed, and the race for wealth eliminated, other objects and ambitions will take the place of the personal struggle for individual material existence; since all will benefit from the labour of all honour will be done, not to the wealthy, as at present, but to those who are skilful and zealous in the common service.

Emulation in work will take the place of emulation in wealth.

With the disappearance of the anxious struggle for existence, which saps the energy and cripples initiative, a new vigour, a new independence will develop. People will have more courage to desire freedom, greater determination to possess it. They will be more exacting in their demands upon life, more fastidious as to their choice of a vocation. They will wish to work at what they enjoy, to order their lives as they desire. Work will be generally enjoyed as never before in the history of mankind.

The desire for freedom will be tempered by the sense of responsibility towards the commonweal, which will provide security for all.

Public opinion provides a stronger, more general compulsion than any penal code, and public opinion will strongly disapprove idleness and waste.

To secure the abundant production necessary to Communism, and to cope with the ever-growing complexity of modern life and requirements, large-scale production and co-operative effort is necessary. The people of today would not be willing to go back to producing everything by hand in domestic workshops; were they to do so, they could not maintain the population in comfort and with reasonable leisure. The people of today would be unwilling to abandon all the productive factories, the trains, the electric generating stations and so on. The retention of such things necessitates the working-together of large numbers of people. As soon as numbers of people are working together and supplying with their products numbers of other people, some sort of organisation of work and of distribution becomes inevitable. The work itself cannot be carried on without organisation. In each industry, either the workers concerned in the work must form and control the organisation, or they will be under the dominion of the organisers. The various industries are interlocked in interest and utility; therefore the industrial organisations must be interlocked.

When wages have disappeared, when all are upon a basis of economic equality, when the position of manager, director, organiser, etc., brings no material advantage, the desire for it will be less widespread and less keen, and the danger of oppressive action by the management will be largely nullified. Nevertheless, management imposed on unwilling subordinates will not be tolerated; where the organiser has chosen the assistants, the assistants will be free to leave, or change him; where the assistants choose the organiser, they will be free to change him. Co-operation for the common good is necessary, but freedom, not domination, is the goal.

Since co-operative work and mutual reliance on mutual aid renders some kind of organisation necessary, the best possible form of organisation must be chosen: the test of its worth is its efficiency and the scope for freedom and initiative it allows to each of its units.

The Soviet structure of committees and delegates, built up from the base of the workshop and village assembly, presents the best form of organisation yet evolved; it arises naturally when the workers are thrown upon their own resources in the matter of government.

The Soviet structure will undoubtedly be the organisational structure of Communism, at any rate for some time to come. We live always, however, in a state of flux, and there is and happily can be, no permanence about human institutions; there is always the possibility of something higher, as yet undiscovered.

The overthrow of Capitalism precedent to the establishment of Communism will be resisted by the possessors of wealth. Thus Capitalism will only be overthrown by revolution.

The revolution can only come when conditions are ripe for it; but opportunities may be missed: the rising may fail to take place at the opportune moment, or it may fail by mismanagement of the proletarian forces. A partial success may be achieved, and if Capitalism is not completely destroyed, it may afterwards re-establish itself, as it speedily did in Hungary, as it is gradually doing in Russia.

Part Two

Workers Dreadnought, December 3rd 1921

Since the overthrow of capitalism would be resisted by the possessors of wealth, whether this were effected by Act of Parliament or by a sudden revolt of the people, it is absolutely necessary for the Communists to prepare the working class for such resistance. Many people still doubt that capitalist resistance to the overthrow of capitalism will go to the length of civil war, yet there is abundant contemporary evidence to prove that such resistance will be made.

Here in Britain we have the Ulster capitalists' preparations for armed resistance to the Asquith Home Rule Act. The civil war threats and preparations by Ulster Capitalism were and are supported by British Toryism. That is why it succeeds. Since British and Ulster landlords and capitalists have thought it worthwhile to resort to the extreme of civil war on the Irish question how absolutely certain it is that they would do so to prevent the establishment of Communism and proletarian rule!

In Finland, in Central Europe, in Russia, the same thing has been seen; when capitalism is in danger capitalism resorts to force of arms to protect itself. In Italy too, the fascisti, with their armed attacks on Communists, Socialists, Trade Unionists, and Co-operators; attacks organised by the Capitalists who use these disorderly bands as their tools, are but another evidence of the same fact: when the established order is in danger its beneficiaries arm to protect it; its supporters and opponents come to blows, civil war breaks out and for the time being peace is no more.

Is that as it should be? It is as it is. The inevitable must be recognised and prepared for. A determined struggle for supremacy inevitably accompanies the overthrow of capitalism.

Experience shows that the crisis arises suddenly: the old relationship has been growing more and more strained, and suddenly the bonds are snapped and the storm bursts. We do not say that a Parliamentary crisis could not be the last straw that would precipitate the revolution, but in none of the contemporary revolutions has this been so. We have now the experience of Russia, Finland, Germany (where there have been a revolution and several attempts at further revolution), in Austria and Hungary to look to.

Great economic pressure, fired by a great rebellion against the actions and ideology of those who have been in power, is the factor which produces the proletarian revolution. Parliament must be overthrown with the capitalist system if the proletarian revolution is to succeed there must be a clean break with the old institutions of Government; the revolution must create its own instrument.

Parliament would have to be sacrificed with the overthrow of capitalism, even were it conceivable that an Act of Parliament will formally abolish the capitalist system. The capitalists would resist by force the first attempt to put the Act into practice, and Parliament is not the body that could carry the proletarian revolution through to success in face of capitalist revolt, which would be one of both armed and passive resistance.

The workers would be compelled to meet such a revolt with all the forces at their disposal; their most characteristic weapon is their industrial power, for the effective wielding of which they would have to be co-ordinated industrially. Every industry would be divided against itself; the owners and part of the management would take the capitalist side, the mass of the workers the side of the working class. As in all the countries where the revolutionary crisis has appeared, the naval and military forces would be divided in the same way, though the old training and discipline would probably cause a larger proportion of the working class rank-and-file to support the side of the master class than would be the case in industry.

A little consideration of such a situation must reveal to anyone who thinks seriously that Parliament and the local governing bodies; the county and borough councils, the boards of guardians, and so on, could not be the guiding and co-ordinating machinery of such a struggle; that such machinery could take no other form than that of the Soviets.

Even in a war between rival capitalist governments Parliament becomes a cipher in the struggle; the machinery that carries out the war is the Cabinet composed of the heads of the various Departments of State, all very much controlled by the expert managers of those departments. On the military side the political and military heads of the War Office work in contact with a machine which is composed of all the officers from the highest to the lowest in the army, and the men under their command. On the industrial side the political and technical heads of the departments work through a machine which is composed of the owners, managers and workers in all industries, factories, workshops.

So it will be in the proletarian revolution, but this being a struggle between the workers and their masters, the officers and the managers will be proletarian leaders chosen by their fellows. And contact with the rank and file will be by delegates and mass meetings. The services of the rank [and] file will not be based on compulsion and wagery, but on consent and enthusiasm and a voice in responsibility for aims and policies.

War experience will show us that even capitalism found that shop stewards and councils on which Trade Union officials co-operated with the management were helpful in securing greater output, which was necessary to their success in war.

Some people may say that the Soviets could be abandoned and Parliament reverted to after the clash of civil war had passed; and that, as they hope there may be no such clash, they will not interest themselves in the question of Soviets. Further consideration should show them, however, that even were hope of avoiding a struggle with capitalism justified, Parliament would have to go and the Soviets would become necessary at least for some time after the overthrow of capitalism.

Consider the position here in London with capitalism abolished; the tubes, trams and buses, the main line stations, the docks, the reservoirs, the gas works, the electric generating stations, the bakeries, food preserving, clothing and other factories, the slaughter-houses, butchers, bakers, greengrocers, grocers and other wholesale and retail shops and the markets. Millions of people are waiting for their daily supply of milk and bread to be brought round to them, to find their daily supply of provender in the shops where they deal, their habitual means of transport. If any of these things stop, then at least some people will not arrive at their daily work, and masses of others may thus be deprived of accustomed necessaries. Perhaps the workers are already engaged in a general strike; perhaps the wheels of industry and transport are already dislocated, and everyone is already living a hungry, makeshift existence.

Whichever way it be, everything has to be reorganised and built up on a new basis; production for use, not for profit, and capitalism is overthrown. Undoubtedly some of those who used to manage the big concerns under the old system have refused to function any more; undoubtedly many others can not be trusted to occupy such important positions of trust; already they have shown their hostility and have taken to sabotage. And there are the people, the hungering millions of all sorts, clamouring to have their wants supplied, each with their peculiarities, their likes and dislikes, their reasonable and unreasonable prejudices, and crowds of them ready to start looting if they are kept waiting or denied what they are accustomed to have and what they think is their due. Everyone, both as worker and consumer, has new hopes and desires and new claims upon life, for has not the Workers' Revolution come? Everyone demands more leisure and more congenial labour, more food, more clothes, more pleasure; only the patient people are prepared to wait, and everyone is

14

finding his daily work, assuming he is prepared to do it as of old, quite dislocated. Everyone, too, is demanding a new independent status, and a share in deciding how things shall be done.

Imagine bringing unfortunate Parliament into such a dilemma. Frank Hodges and T.C. Cramp besieged by a mob of Westminster housewives who cannot obtain either fish or butter. Will Thorne, who is told the electricity supply is cut off in all the suburbs. Ramsay Macdonald, some of whose constituents are tramping to London to tell him that Leicester can get no coal.

The only chance for that Parliament would be to call the Industrial Soviets into being!

As to the borough councils: we remember the little matter of the food rationing, and the groups of housewives here and there who, through the muddles of the local food committee and the Ministry of Food, found themselves as "outlanders" prohibited from buying at the shops where they had hitherto dealt, and unable to procure commodities anywhere else.

The only people who could deal with the great new situation would be the people who do the work and the people who use the produce. All interlocked as they are in this busy hive of overcrowded life the Soviets would be the only solution. The workers in the factory in a turmoil of dislocation would come together and talk the matter over; appoint one of their number to answer the telephone, another to fetch supplies; others to take stock; others, according to their capacities, to mind the various machines, others to acquaint the absentees that the factory is at work again, others as organisers and instructors. They would send to the workers in other factories for more supplies and organise exchanges.

The women rushing frantically about in search of supplies, and threatening to start looting and rioting because their children are hungry, would be called together by the more level-headed, would enumerate their wants and place their demands before the workers responsible for production and transport.

Part Three

Workers Dreadnought December 10 1921

In Russia all this was done, and over vast districts, under the spur of need without preliminary thought or organisation.

In this country the workers cannot leave things to chance. Capitalism is highly organised here and will defeat the workers' revolution again and again, unless the workers are organised efficiently. Moreover, in London and in the vast chains of towns which form our industrial districts we are so closely massed on the ground, so absolutely dependent on food brought in from outside, and upon the collective service of the whole industrial community, that unless production and distribution is well organised we must speedily starve.

It will go hard with us if we have not created the machinery before the hour of revolution strikes.

The machinery of the Soviets must obviously follow, and does so far as it is successful, the lines of need. Each workshop has its meetings and elects its delegates to a factory committee. The factory will also have its mass meetings of all workers on occasion. Every factory will be united to the factories of the same industry in the district through its committee of delegates, and in the same way will be co-ordinated with every factory in the same industry in the country. These are the bodies which will meet and discuss what concerns the industry, but for matters which concern the district in which the workers live and work they will go to mass meetings or send delegates to committees from all the industries in the district. The housekeepers will have their own meetings also, and they, too, will go to mass meetings or send delegates to the producing industries when arrangements are to be made between them.

All this will be done purely by way of managing affairs so that all may be, as far as possible, satisfied that the needs of all may be explained and understood by those who have to supply them.

But there should be no compulsion; some people may say: "What the majority decide is good enough for me." Others will say: "I like to have a voice in it." As a rule, when things affecting a group of people who are working together come up for decision everyone of the group will join in and give his or her opinion, and generally the thing will be decided by mutual agreement.

The Dictatorship of the Proletariat

The dictatorship of the proletariat is a much misused phrase; when Communism is in being there will be no proletariat, as we understand the term today, and no dictatorship.

The dictatorship, so far as it is genuine and defensible, is the suppression by Workers' Soviets of capitalism and the attempt to re-establish it. This should be a temporary state of war. Such a period will inevitably occur, we believe, because we do not believe that the possessors of wealth will submit to the overthrow of capitalism without resistance. On the contrary, [we] believe the owners will fight to preserve capitalism by every means in their power.

Whilst the capitalists are openly fighting the workers who have seized the power, fighting them openly and secretly in armed battalions in guerilla bands, by ambush assasination bombs, sabotage, spies; then the proletariat must maintain a vigilant war service and dictatorship. The situation in Ireland before the truce is a little like what a proletarian dictatorship may have to cope with.

Once, however, the war is over, once the capitalist and his allies have given up any serious attempt to re-establish capitalism, then away with dictatorship; away with compulsion.

Compulsion of any kind is repugnant to the Communist ideal. No-one may make a wage-slave of another; no-one may hoard up goods for himself that he does not require and cannot use; but the only way to prevent such practices is not by making them punishable; it is by creating a society in which no-one needs to become a wage slave, and no-one cares to be cumbered with a private hoard of goods when all that he needs is readily supplied as he needs it from the common storehouse.

Compulsory education for children has been a protection for children in this capitalist society when parents are poor and grasping enough to desire the earnings of their children or to suffer from the burden of their maintenance, but when all things that nature and mankind produce are free in abundance for the asking what parents would deny education to their children; what children would submit with the school-door freely open?

Part Four

Workers Dreadnought December 24th 1921 and January 21st 1922

We have seen that the Soviets are destined both to provide the organisational machinery of Communist society and to act as the instrument of the proletarian dictatorship during the transitional period in which, whilst capitalism has been overthrown, the dispossessed owners have not yet settled down to accept the new order. The Soviets may also conduct the fight for the actual overthrow of Capitalism, though in Russia the power was actually seized by the Bolshevik Party; then handed to the Soviets.

Let us consider the essential structure of the Soviet, its particular characteristic, wherein lies its special fitness to function as the administrative machinery of the Communist community.

The Soviet is constructed along the lines of production and distribution; it replaces not merely Parliament and the present local governing bodies, but also the capitalists, managerial staffs and employees of today with all their ramifications. The functional units of the Soviets are the groups of workers of all grades, including those engaged in management in the factory, the dockyard, the mine, the farm, the warehouse, the office, the distributive store, the school, the hospital, the printing shop, the laundry, the restaurant, and the domestic workers in the communal household, the street or block of dwellings.

The generally accepted theoretical structure of the Soviet community is as follows:

Industrial Co-ordination

The Workshop Committee: comprising all the workers in the shop.

The Factory Committee: comprising delegates from the Workshop Committees.

The District Committee: comprising delegates from the factory or sub-district committees of the workers in the industry, and from district committees of distributive workers engaged in distributing the products of the industry.

The National Committee: composed of delegates from district committees.

Inter-industrial Co-ordination

District and Sub-District Committees: Delegates from district or sub district committees of industries (including factories, docks, farms, laundries, restaurants, centres of distribution, schools, domestic workers, parks, theatres, etc., workers in all branches of social activity being represented).

National Committee: comprising delegates of district committees of all industries and works of social activity.

Thus there is a dual machinery: 1. For the organisation and co-ordination of each industry and social activity; 2. for the linking together of all industries and social activities.

The network of committees of delegates which makes up the framework of the Soviets and links the many productive groups, and also individual producers should not be regarded as a rigid, cast-iron machinery, but as a convenient means of transacting necessary business, a practical method of inter-organisation which gives everyone the opportunity of a voice in social management. The members of a community are dependent upon each other. The cotton spinning mill is operated by a number of groups of workers practising various crafts. The workers in the spinning mill are dependent for the execution of their work on the cotton growers, the railwaymen, the mariners, and the dockers, who provide them with the raw material of their trade. They are dependent on machine makers, miners, electricians and others for the machinery of spinning and the power to run it, and on the weaver, the bleacher, the dyer, the printer, the garment worker and upholsterer to complete the work they have begun. In order that the spinners may do their work they are also dependent on builders, decorators, furniture makers, food producers, garment makers, and innumerable others whose labours are necessary to maintain them in health and efficiency.

At present it is the employer who directs, the merchant who co-ordinates and distributes social production. When capitalism is destroyed another medium of direction, co-ordination and distribution must be discovered, the productive processes must not fall into chaos. The Soviets will supply the necessary medium of co-ordination and direction; but they must become a medium of convenience, not of compulsion; otherwise there can be no genuine Communism.

In Russia the Soviet constitution has only been very partially applied, and has not been theoretically regular in structure, and is still constantly subject to large modifications.

The Russian Soviets had not been created in advance in preparation for the revolution of March, 1917: they sprang into life in the time of crisis. They had arisen in the revolution of 1905, but had died away at its fall. The March, 1917, revolution only created Soviets in a few centres, and though their number grew and was added to by the November Bolshevik revolution, even yet the network of Soviets is incomplete. Kameneff, reporting on this question to the seventh all-Russian Congress of Soviets in 1920, stated that even where Soviets existed their general assemblies were often rare, and when held frequently only listened to a few speeches and dispersed without transacting any real business.

Nevertheless, the Soviet government had claimed that the number of Soviets actually functioning has grown continuously; yet it freely admits that the Soviets have taken neither so active nor so responsible a part as they should in the creation and management of the new community. Russia's "new economic policy" of reversion to capitalism strikes at the root of the Soviet idea and destroys the functional status of the Soviets.

Russia's special difficulties in applying the Soviet system were inherent in the backward state of the country which had only partially progressed from feudalism into capitalism. In industry the small home producer still accounted for 60 per cent of Russia's industrial production. In agriculture the peasants had not yet been divorced from the land as is the case in England, where we have long had a completely landless class of rural workers. In Russia the ideal of the land worker was to produce for himself on his own holding and to sell his products, not to work in co-operation with others. The Russian peasants, vastly outnumbering the rest of the population, were all but unanimous in their demands. Those who had no land were determined to get a piece for themselves, and those who had a little piece of land wanted more. Though their individualism was tempered by the old custom of periodically re-dividing the land and other village traditions, the peasants were an influence against Communism. Nevertheless, their ancient village council, the Mir, a survival from the period of primitive Communism, had somewhat prepared them for the Soviets.

In the scattered village communities the occupational character of the Soviet is apparently somewhat submerged in the territorial; yet all the subsidiary crafts of the villages are attendant on the great industry of agriculture. Ties of common interest and mutual dependence, which are the life-blood of the Soviet, are clearly apparent between the land workers and the various craftsmen of the village. The blurring of the occupational character of the village Soviet does not detract from its function of an administrative unit in harmony with the actual conditions of the country. On the other hand, the fact that the town Soviets could not supply it with the industrial products it needed, by weakening the link of mutual usefulness, making the usefulness merely one-sided, removed the natural impetus of the Soviets of the villages to link themselves for utilitarian reasons with the Soviets of the towns. Production by individual producers who are competing with each other creates sources of conflict which are antagonistic to the Soviet. The strongest and most useful Soviet must always be that which is formed of those who are working together and who realise at every turn that they are dependent on each other. The necessity for the Soviet becomes more pronounced and its work more varied the more that work is carried on in common and the more closely the lives of the people are related to each other. Mankind is gregarious; the degree of gregariousness in human beings is partly dependant on material conditions, partly on inclination (which is doubtless largely, if not wholly, the slow product of long environment). As humanity secures a completer mastery over matter, individual choice as to how life shall be spent, becomes broader and more free; science will more and more enable desire to determine the degree of industrial concentration. Our civilisation has perhaps nearly reached the limit of the tendency to gather together ever greater and greater numbers of workers, performing some tiny mechanical operation as attendants to machinery. Perhaps the future has in store for us an entirely opposite development. That would not effect the fact that the Soviet must find its most congenial soil in a society based on mutual aid and mutual dependence.

In the industrial centres where it might have been expected that the occupational basis of the Soviet would have been adhered to, the structure of the Russian Soviets was irregular from the theoretical standpoint. The Soviets, instead of being formed purely of workers in the various industries and activities of the community, were composed also of delegates of political parties, political groups formed by foreigners in Russia,

23

Trades Councils, Trade Unions and co-operative societies. Pravda of April 18th, 1918, published the following regulations for the Moscow Soviet elections:—

"Regulations for Representation.

"Establishments employing 200 to 500 workers, one representative; those employing over 500, send one representative for every 500 men. Establishments employing less than 200 workers, combine for purpose of representation with other small establishments.

"Ward Soviets send two deputies, elected at a plenary session.

"Trade Unions with a membership not exceeding 2,000, send one deputy; not exceeding 5,000, two deputies; above 5,000, one for every 5,000 workers, but not more than ten deputies for any one union.

"The Moscow Trades' Council sends five deputies.

"Political parties send 30 deputies to the Soviet: the seats are allotted to the parties in proportion to their membership, providing the parties include four representatives of industrial establishments and organised workers.

"Representatives of the following National non-Russian Socialist parties, one representative per party, are allotted seats:—

(a) "Bund" (Jewish).
(b) Polish Socialist Party (Left).
(c) Polish and Lithuanian Social Democratic Parties.
(d) Lettish Social Democratic Party.
(e) Jewish Social Democratic Party."

The intention in giving representation to these various interests was, of course, to disarm their antagonism to the Soviet power and to secure their co-operation instead; but the essential administrative character of the Soviets was thereby sacrificed. Constituted thus they must inevitably discuss political antagonisms rather than the production and distribution of social utilities and amenities.

The industrial unions, economic councils and co-operative societies which have been a feature of Soviet Russia (the two former having representation in the Soviets) have no place, because they have no reason for existence, under an efficient Soviet system, in which they would be absorbed into the occupational Soviets and indistinguishably fused with them.

Industrial unions can have no reason for existence if the Soviets are fulfilling efficiently their proper function as the administrative machinery of the Communist community, for the Soviets should cover the same constituencies as the industrial unions. The industrial unions will only exist so long as there is either a conflict between the workers and the Soviets (which are theoretically the organs of the workers), or in case the Soviets are failing to administer industry or administer it efficiently. The very existence of the Industrial Union, unless it be merely a social club, denotes an antagonism between the members of the union and those who are administering industry; unless, on the other hand, the Soviets are failing to administer industry and the unions are formed for that purpose. In Russia, as a matter of fact, the continued existence of the industrial unions is due to the fact that there it antagonism between the workers and those who are administering industry. In a theoretically correct Soviet community the workers, through their Soviets, which are indistinguishable from them, should administer. This has not been achieved in Russia.

Co-operatives have no place in a genuine Soviet community. If they are distributive organisations purely, they should be the distributive branches of the industrial Soviets. If they are organs of buying and selling, they are survivals of capitalism and must disappear under Communism. If they are associations of producers they can only differ from industrial

Soviets in so far as they exact payment in cash or kind for their produce instead of distributing it freely. In so far as they exact payment or practice barter, they have no place in a Soviet community.

The curious overlapping patchwork which has hitherto made up the Russian Soviet system should by no means be slavishly copied. The Russians themselves have emphasised that. Nevertheless, the recent tactics which they have induced the Third International to adopt do not indicate that they have a clear perception that a highly organised industrial community may build the new Communist order on the theoretically correct foundation of the occupational Soviets.

Part Five

Workers Dreadnought January 28th 1922

Zinoviev, at the Second Congress of the Third International in Moscow, introduced a Thesis declaring that no attempt should be made to form Soviets prior to the outbreak of the revolutionary crisis. It was argued that, as such bodies would be powerless, or nearly so, their formation might bring the conception of the Soviets into proletarian contempt. The Thesis was adopted by the Congress, without discussion, and thereby became an axiom of the Third International.

The question as to whether the mere borrowed term, Soviet, shall be reserved for use in the actual crisis of revolution is of small importance though, if not used previously, it would probably miss being adopted as the slogan of the revolution.

The question of postponing the creation of the actual organisation till the hour of a revolutionary crisis is, on the other hand, a fundamental one.

The idea expressed and insisted upon in that Thesis of Zinoviev's was that the Soviet must be a great mass movement, coming together in the electrical excitement of the crisis; the correctness of its structure, its actual Sovietness (to coin an adjective), being considered of secondary importance. A progressive growth, gradually branching out till the hour of crisis; a strong and well-tried organisation is not contemplated by the Thesis. The need for carefully conceived structure is ignored. Propaganda for the Soviets alone is recommended.

Russia's dual Revolution was an affair of spontaneous outbursts, with no adequate organisation behind it. The Trade Unions, always a feeble growth, were crushed by the Czardom at the outbreak of the great war of 1914. The Revolutionary political parties could call for a revolution; they could not carry it through: that was accomplished by the action of the revolutionary elements in the Army and Navy, in the workshops, on the railways, and on the land. That these revolutionaries at the point of production were mainly unorganised was a disability, not an advantage. In Russia the government first of the Czar, then of Kerensky, crumbled readily under the popular assault. The disability arising from the disorganised state of the workers was not felt in its full weightiness until after the Soviet Government had been established. Then it was realised that, though the Soviets were supposed to have taken power, the Soviet structure had yet to be created and made to function. The structure is still incomplete: it has functioned hardly at all. Administration has been largely by Government departments, working often without the active, ready co-operation, sometimes even with the hostility of groups of workers who ought to have been taking a responsible share in administration. To this cause must largely be attributed Soviet Russia's defeat on the economic front.

It would be monstrous folly for workers in other countries, especially in highly industrialised countries where Capitalism is old, to imitate Russia's unpreparedness. We in Britain have an infinitely stronger Capitalism to overturn: we have greater opportunities of creating the organisation necessary to fight it.

This organisation must be able both to attack and destroy Capitalism in the final struggle, and also to replace the administrative machinery of Capitalism. Moreover it must be animated by the will to these achievements.

We have at present no such organisation in this country.

Our Trade Unions have neither the will, nor the capacity for the purpose. We are nearest industrial unionism in mining and transport and on the land, but even there we have several competing Unions in each industry. In the textile, metal, food preparing, wood-working, clothing, and building industries, we have a multiplicity of little-co-ordinated organisations. Moreover, the great mass of the workers is divided into two sections: the skilled and the unskilled: organised into quite separate Unions and divided by impassable barriers which have been jealously erected and maintained by the skilled workers.

The structure of the Trade Unions is antiquated and fruitful of delays. It is highly undemocratic, some Unions have first and second class members, the former, of ten or more years' standing, alone being eligible for office; some elect their executive for eight years or some other long term; some hold no general congress of branch representatives. The rank and file members of the Unions have little or no voice in deciding the larger issues of policy. The executive usually determining the policy to be pursued at national conferences with other bodies. The rules, which are registered with the capitalist Government's Registrar General, cannot be changed without long and hard effort. Under normal circumstances it must take many years to change them appreciably. The rules and structure of the Unions would place a handicap upon any serious attempt that might be made to remould the Unions in order that they might function with some sort of efficiency in the attack on Capitalism and in the administration of industry after Capitalism were overthrown.

The rules and structure are even a serious handicap in the daily struggle to palliate Capitalism, which is what the Unions exist for.

The Union officials who, almost to a man, desire the retention of the capitalist system, fear, above all things, any serious attack upon it, are aided and protected in their conservatism by the Union rules.

The reactionary officials have, however, a stronger buttress and protection in the backward masses, who vastly outnumber the awakened workers in the Trade Unions. It is only in the advanced stages of the Revolution that the great masses will discern the gulf between themselves and their reactionary leaders. This is one of the reasons why another organisation is necessary. Such an organisation must reveal to the masses the true character of their leaders, and offer them an alternative policy.

The Trade Unions are composed of masses of workers who did not become members of the Unions with the object of changing the social system, but merely to palliate it. Latterly men and women have even been forced into the Unions, because Trade Unions had become strong enough to insure that those who refused to join would have difficulty in obtaining employment. With such a membership, the Trade Unions are naturally timid, conservative bodies, apt to oppose drastic change and unready to take any bold initiative.

We believe that such Trade Unions can never deliberately precipitate a revolution. In this matter, theory is supported by experience. In Russia the revolution was not made by the hardly-existing Trade Unions. After the first revolution the Central Council of Soviets laboured to form Trade Unions. Some of the Unions it had formed then opposed retention of power by the Soviets, worked against all tendencies towards Communism, and gave their support to the demand for a bourgeois republic, with Capitalism re-established in power.

In Germany, the Trade Unions, so far from leading the various proletarian uprisings, took no official part except to oppose them.

To administer in place of Capitalism, as well as to overthrow it, the workers should be organised with all, and more than all, the efficiency and coherence of Capitalism. In this country, Capitalism itself, though tremendously better equipped than in Russia under the Czardom, still lacks co-ordination. As a medium for supplying the people's needs, it suffers on the one hand from the competition and overlapping of private interests; and, on the other, from shortage and lack in districts where the small means of the people do not render it profitable to supply them efficiently. Every day British Capitalism is remedying some of its organisational defects, at least, some of those due to its own internal capitalist rivalries.

From banking, where we have nearly arrived at a single trust, to tea-shops, where Lyons is absorbing competitor after competitor, co-ordination and the elimination of competition is going on constantly. Trustification has not yet developed nearly so far in Britain as in Germany, where the combination of the powerful capitalist, Stinnes, links up coal and ore mining, smelting, and the manufacture, shipping and marketing of all sorts of metal goods; forestry, wood-working, paper-making, printing and publishing; tram, train, and sea travel, and the provision of hotel accommodation; the production and supply of electricity in all its branches, and a host of other activities.

British Capitalist organisation will rapidly become more closely knit under pressure of the competition which is rising up against it all over the world: in Britain's own colonies and dominions, in America, in the growing industrialism of Poland, Italy, and other European countries, above all in Germany, whose Capitalism, still more since the war that was meant to crush it, is Britain's keenest rival.

We should welcome the trustification of industry, in so far as it is a co-ordination along the lines of convenience and utility in producing and distributing what is needed by the populace. We should welcome it also because it provides the means of linking up the workers into a closely-knit fighting organisation; an organisation which can step in and displace the capitalist, and, having done so, shall be able to carry on production and distribution.

Such an organisation may be built up by organising the workers in the co-ordinated centres of production and distribution along the lines of the Trust itself. The Trade Unions are not thus organised.

Although Trustification has not yet developed very far in

Britain, British employers of labour are much better organised than British workers. Employers' Associations and Trade Journals bind the employers together in all industries, and a much greater degree of solidarity is shown by the employing class than by the working class when a trade dispute arises. In this country Trade Unionism has never achieved the general strike: it has even shrunk from attempting any large-scale sympathetic strike. In this respect British Trade Unionism is behind that of most European countries. Both ideologically and structurally it is distinctly outdistanced by its continental contemporaries. Indeed, it is solely on the size of its membership that the British Trade Union movement has claimed to be the strongest in the world. As a body of action it would gain in strength if it could be ruthlessly pruned of its more backward members.

The trustification and co-ordination of industry under Capitalism has for many years been causing a perpetual discussion upon industrial unionism to be carried on in the Labour movement; but the result in actual improvements in the Union structure has been surprisingly small.

That rapid wartime growth, the Shop Stewards' organisation, in a few months co-ordinated the workers in the munition factories and shipyards with an efficient completeness the Trade Unions had never approached, and made the Stewards' movement a coherent acting force, such as the Trade Unions had never been. This development shows that the task of organising the workers in accordance with Capitalist organisation, in which the Trade Unions have hitherto failed, may readily be accomplished by building upon a new basis, unhindered by the trammels of the old machinery and the prejudices and vested interests of the old officials.

It may, perhaps, be objected that since the Shop Stewards' organisation dwindled at the close of the war and has all but passed away, there are elements of permanency in the Trade Unions which the Shop Stewards did not possess. That is true. The Trade Unions remained in possession of their accumulated funds, and were adding to these funds week by week, for the workers continued paying their Trade Union dues week by week; although the Trade Unions were functioning only as benefit societies, whilst the rank and file workers themselves were doing, through their shop committees and their elected stewards, the work for which the Unions were created. The Unions retained possession of the funds and the friendly benefits. When the boom in production passed and unemployment became rife in the land, the workers unready for the time being to safeguard their status in the workshop, were glad to fall back on the friendly benefits of the Union.

Part Six

Workers Dreadnought February 4th 1922

As we have seen, the main purpose of the Soviets is to minister to the needs of the people, in clothing, housing, education, recreation, transport and so on. The workers who are responsible for these services are linked together in their Soviets for the purposes of their work. The Soviet structure is efficient, because it is formed on the lines necessitated by the work; also because it gives every worker a responsible share in the common effort, and thereby encourages the co-operative impulse. Even under Capitalism the merits of the workshop council, which is the germ of the Soviet, have been discovered, not only by the workers, but by the capitalist himself. During the war, when the Shop Stewards' Movement flourished, employers actually initiated the formation of shop councils and the election of workers' stewards.

The employers did so, not merely to forestall the rebel elements, but rather because, in the great stress of war-time and with a tremendous influx of new workers, the shop council organisation would minimise the cost of management, reduce the number of paid supervisors required, and the difficulty of maintaining discipline, and increase the output by producing a spirit of willingness amongst the workers who were responsive to the patriotic appeals to produce more.

Mr. Charles Reynold, of the big engineering firm of that name, recently gave an address on workshop committees and the control of industry: he described how the works committee at his firm holds monthly meetings with the management to discuss wages and conditions of labour, and all questions of management. He declared that the confidential financial information presented to the directors is communicated to the works committee, and the result is the creation of a sense of responsibility, an understanding of the management point of view, and the acceptance of changes with comparatively little friction.

From the class-war standpoint this information does not gratify us, and presumably the scheme is part of some profit-sharing arrangement. It is nevertheless testimony to the value of the workshop council from the administrative efficiency standpoint, although under Capitalism the shop council has, of course, no real power, and only a leading-strings share of responsibility. Reynold's is but one of many capitalist firms which are endeavouring, in the interests of efficiency, to secure the co-operation of their workers, though capitalist conditions prevent the co-operation from being genuine on either side. The growth of Whitleyism shows that the intelligent British capitalists are beginning to understand that men and women only give their best when they give of their free will, feeling that they are responsible entities. This truth is too often forgotten by those who once preached it, when they attain to official positions, whether in Russia, or in Britain.

The trend of the times supports the view that the Soviet Government made a serious blunder when it decided (and put into practice its decision) that "workers' control of industry" is only a slogan useful for securing the overthrow of the capitalist, and must be discarded, once the workers have turned out the capitalist, in favour of management by an individual or committee appointed by some centralised authority.

A careful and candid survey of the Russian attempt to establish Communism will some day reveal, more clearly than at present, the proportional weight of the causes which have led to its failure. That it has failed for the present, and that only a powerful new impetus can stop the present retrogression in Russia we are compelled to admit.

Such a candid survey will provide evidence as to how far the Russian failure has been due to the capitalist resistance to

Communism; how far to the unreadiness of the population; how far to the mistakes of the Communists, and especially to the mistakes of the Soviet Government.

The question of workers' control of industry will bulk largely in this connection.

Viewed from the standpoint of efficiency as a fighting force, it is notorious that never were strikes so swiftly, solidly and successfully effected in this country as those of the war-time Shop Stewards' movement. A rank and file chorus complaining of the inefficiency, inactivity and lack of class solidarity shown by the reactionary Trade Union leaders is constantly rising and falling. During the Dublin Lock-Out of 1912, during the railway strike of 1919 and the coal strike of 1921, it swelled with indignation, but only the workers organised in the workshop committees have taken large-scale action, except at the bidding of the Union officials. This is not unnatural: until both the individual workers and the workers in each individual firm feel that others will act with them, they shrink from taking action which, if not supported, will lead to their victimisation.

To recapitulate: the Soviets, or workers' occupational councils, will form the administrative machinery for supplying the needs of the people in Communist society; they will also make the revolution by seizing control of all the industries and services of the community.

Though in Russia the revolution was accomplished by Soviets which sprang up spontaneously in some places and by unorganised mob risings, this was only possible, because the government of Russia had broken down, Capitalism was weak and of limited extent, and the entire country in a state of chaotic disorder.

Here in Britain the machinery of the Soviets must be prepared in advance. In all the industries and services, revolutionary workers, who are habitually at work there and know the ropes, must be prepared to seize and maintain control.

The Trade Unions do not provide this machinery: they are not competent, either to seize, control, or to administer industry. They are not structurally fitted to administer industry, because their organisations do not combine all the workers in any industry, and they are not efficiently co-ordinated. Their branches are constructed according to the district in which the worker resides, not according to where he works.

The Trade Unions are, moreover opposed to revolutionary action: their object is to secure palliations of the capitalist system, not to abolish it.

British experience has shown that the workers' council system is efficient both as an engine for fighting the employer, and as a means of administrating the industry. Experience has also shown that under favourable conditions it can be built up with remarkable rapidity.

Experience in those European countries where the workers and their organisations have been tested in the revolutionary fight, has shown that the workers' council is always the organ of the workers' struggle. The Trade Unions, having tried unsuccessfully to avert the contest, in each case threw the weight of their influence on to the side of preserving the established order, and opposed every effort of the workers and their councils to overpower the employing class.

The evidence given by J.H. Thomas in his libel case against the Communist and its officials reveals the attitude which he will adopt in the event of any struggles for Proletarian power in this country. J.H. Thomas must not be regarded as an exception: the British Trade Union officials will all adopt the same attitude. Some will denounce the revolutionary workers on platforms, openly proclaiming their allegiance to the Crown, the Government and the employing class; others will merely hold aloof from the revolutionaries and in the Trade Union conferences will vote against the Unions joining the revolutionaries in the struggle. If they do not advise Trade Union members to give actual assistance to the Government in coercing the revolutionaries, they will at least advise their members to assist the cause of re-establishing the disturbed capitalist order by remaining quietly at work — the obedient servants of the capitalist employer, or of the capitalist Government.

This is the part which the Trade Unions and their officials have played in every one of the many recent proletarian uprisings in other countries: this is the part which J.H. Thomas and his colleagues will play here. J.H. Thomas differs only in degree from his colleagues who belong to the Reformist School. The British Trade Union movement and its officials belong to the same school as the Trade Unions and Trade Union officials of Europe and America.

The Trade Unions have too loose and uncoordinated a structure to make the revolution: they are ideologically opposed to it: therefore they will fight it.

The workers' councils, co-ordinated industrially and nationally along the lines of production and distribution, are the organs which are structurally fitted to give the workers greatest power in the control of industry. If that power is to be used to overthrow the present system, the councils, which together will form a "One Big Union" of workers' committees in all industries, should be built, from the first, with the object of taking control.

In Germany, where the methods necessary for waging the proletarian struggle are being forged during the struggle, the Revolutionary Workers' Union, the A.A.U., is a fighting force which has had to be reckoned with. Its growth has been accelerated by the fact that the reactionary Trade Unions have expelled their revolutionary members.

Part Seven

Workers Dreadnought March 11th 1922

The great task of the Communist revolution is ideologic. Communism entails the creation of an altogether new attitude of mind towards all social relationships, and the development of a host of new habits and impulses. In discarding our purse and our financial anxieties and calculations, in removing the dependence of the propertiless upon the propertied, we shall change the entire configuration of life. Communism will create for us a great fraternity, a great trustfulness, arising from a great security, an abundant enthusiasm for productive labour, because such labour will benefit all, and all will share responsibility for it.

Communism necessitates the creation of a great initiative, which shall animate the entire people.

Under Capitalism the masses are as a flock of sheep driven by their owners. Under Communism, on the contrary, they will be free co-operators, producing, inventing, studying, not under the compulsion of law, or poverty, or the incentive of individual gain, but from deliberate choice and with an eager zest for achievement. Communism will provide the material and spiritual conditions which will make voluntary co-operative labour possible. Only by willing service and intelligent initiative can true Communism develop.

The establishment of the Communist life entails a complete breach, both in practice and in ideas, with Capitalism and its machinery. The Parliamentary system is the characteristic machinery of the capitalist State; it has grown up with great similarity in all the countries which have built up their own capitalism. In countries where an alien Capitalism dominates the native populace, the Parliamentary system of the dominant aliens extends the tentacles of its power to the subject country. It sends its officials overseas to rule the natives, entirely discarding its pretended dependence on the consent of the governed and its boasted representative character.

Parliament has been in large measure the co-operative society of the landlords and capitalists through which they have policed the proletariat at home and maintained their power abroad.

The great landlords originally used lawless force and violence for seizing their estates. In the latter half of the fifteenth century they, as feudal lords, drove the peasants, who had the same feudal right to the land as they, from their holdings. The feudal lords usurped the lands which were held and used in common. These things they did in defiance of law and custom, and without waiting to obtain the assent or assistance of Parliament.

Later on, however, the feudal lords found it convenient to give Parliamentary sanction to their robbery of the peasants, and to enact legislation to complete their usurpation of the land. Sitting in Parliament, the lords proceeded thereafter to abolish their own merely feudal tenure of the land, and by creating the modern right of private property in land, they made themselves its absolute owners.

Before they had legalised the expropriation of the peasants, the lords in Parliament enacted legislation to force the peasants they were driving from the land to become their wage-slaves. From the reign of Henry VII, legislation began for the coercion of the dispossessed. We all know that for begging, or wandering without means of subsistence, the landless people were whipped and branded, their ears were sliced, and on a third arrest they were executed. An Act of Edward VI condemned the idler to be the slave of whoever denounced him. He could be sold, bequeathed, or hired as a slave. Any-one might make slaves of his children. Vagabonds, as the dispossessed were called, might be made into parish slaves, condemned to labour for the inhabitants. Only in the reign of Anne, when an industrial proletariat sufficient for the needs of farmers and manufacturers had been developed, were such statutes repealed. So long ago as 1349, Parliament, in the Statute of Labourers, fixed maximum wages to prevent the proletariat from asserting itself to the inconvenience of the employing classes. Maximum wage legislation was maintained thereafter as long as any serious tendency to labour scarcity could give the workers a powerful lever in forcing up their wages.

Parliament has remained the employers' co-operative society for dragooning the workers, in spite of all the extensions of the franchise which have taken place. When a serious labour scarcity arose in our time, during the great European war of 1914-19, Parliament enacted the Munitions Act, to prevent the workers taking advantage of the situation.

Neither in this present period of great unemployment, nor at any other time in history, has Parliament fixed maximum wages to protect the workers when the employers have been taking advantage of a Labour surplus to depress the wages of their employees below the subsistence level. The rates of wages fixed by the Agricultural Wages Boards during the war, were, in reality, a method of attaining by subtle means, the object which the Munitions Act achieved in other industries: namely a check on the bargaining power of Labour during a period of unexampled labour scarcity.

From the early laws against the industrial combination of the workers (maintained by the coercive power of the state as long as the ruling classes considered them necessary) down to our modern D.O.R.A. and E.P.A. and the strike-breaking machinery employed by the government in the last railway and mining strikes, Parliamentary Government has never failed to protect the possessions of the landlords and capitalists, and to employ whatever coercive measures have been necessary to provide the landlords and capitalists with disciplined workers.

41

Parliament and its accessories have been fashioned by the ruling classes for their service. The Courts of Law are strongholds of tradition and privilege, and appointment to the judicial Bench is made obscurely and arbitrarily by the Government.

In case of dispute, the Government-appointed irremovable judges interpret the Parliament-made law. The Government-hired prosecutor — who may even be a member of the Government, is leagued with the Government-appointed judge against the accused. All the force of the Government police assists the prosecution. In political trials, acquittals are remarkably rare. The judges, drawn from the privileged class, almost invariably decide against the popular cause.

The local governing bodies have no power to legislate or initiate: they merely administer the Acts of Parliament under the cramping supervision of Government Departments, which make rules interpreting the Acts of Parliament. Either with, or without Parliamentary sanction, Government departments determine what the local authorities shall spend, by limiting their power to levy Rates and to contract loans, and by prohibiting them from trading, except by special permission of the Government.

As to Parliament itself, its powers have been almost all annexed by the Cabinet.

The King, who is supposed to obey the Government, decides when Parliament shall assemble. The Government decides what subjects Parliament shall discuss, and on what it shall legislate. The Government drafts the legislation. If a measure be amended in a manner displeasing to the Government, the Government withdraws the measure, and either drops it altogether, or re-introduces it in another form. Parliament cannot proceed with any measure unless the Government desire it.

The Speaker and Chairman of Committee appointed by the Government, control the debate and interpret the rules of procedure. Parliamentary discipline is exceedingly strict. No one may speak until called upon by the Speaker, or Chairman of Committee, and the Speaker, or Chairman, may stop any speech, and even prevent the asking of a question, on the ground, either that it is out of order or "it is not in the public interest" that a reply be given. There is no appeal from the ruling of the Chair, which is enforced by the officials of the House, who at once eject any Member failing to obey the Chair.

The Government must have a majority in the House of Commons, or it cannot remain in power. That majority is composed of Party hacks with no chance of being returned to Parliament, except by the aid of the Party machinery and funds. They will not vote against the Government, because to do so would be to incur the ostracism of the Party leaders, and consequently of the Party; such ostracism would inevitably mean the loss of their Parliamentary seats at the next election. The Party man who disobeys his Party must either retire from politics, or become a candidate of the opposite Party (if it will have him, which may not be the case). Many years have passed since a Government was turned out by a hostile Parliamentary vote of its supporters. Even its political opponents are apt to shrink from defeating a Government on a critical issue, which would mean its resignation, for that in most cases entails a General Election. A General Election is of all things that which is most detested by the average Member of Parliament. It means for him an election campaign of tremendous exertion, in which he is compelled to speak at an extraordinary number of meetings, besides canvassing voters and calling on people of influence. Moreover, he may lose his seat, and thus suffer the defeat of many of his ambitions, as well as the loss of an income of four hundred pounds a year. The Member of Parliament prepared to take a line independent of his Party on any subject of importance is exceedingly rare. He is soon eliminated from Parliament.

The Prime Minister is chosen by the Sovereign from amongst the most prominent leaders of the Party which gains the majority of the Parliamentary seats in the General Election.

Persons of powerful influence, of course, make representations to the Sovereign, and the Party caucus and its rival big-wigs all put in their word. What private understandings and guarantees are exacted the people do not know. The Sovereign appoints the rest of the Cabinet on the advice of the Prime Minister, who is influenced, of course, by the powerful personages who provide Party funds, who control Party newspapers, and who are powerful in banking and other circles able to sabotage the Government activities. The wire-pulling and intrigue that surround the making of Cabinets have only been slightly revealed in the memoirs of some of the privileged few who have been behind the scenes.

The policies of Government Departments are supposed to be controlled in general outline by the Cabinet as a whole, and in fuller detail by the Minister at the head of each Department who is appointed by the Prime Minister. The Departments are vast and deal with vast work; the Cabinet of party hacks and political adventurers knows little of the Departments. The responsible Minister, who usually remains in a particular Department no more than a year or two at most, and often no more than a few months, rarely learns much about his work; the permanent officials are the real masters of the administrative detail, and their policy is broadly that of the prevailing capitalist opinion current at the time. Lavish extravagance on Departmental expenditure, and ruthless parsimony towards the people, the great unofficial, unprivileged masses, who are treated as tiresome mendicants, is the outstanding characteristic of administration by Government Departments.

Members of Parliament know little of the doings of Government Departments. The debates, held twice or thrice a year, and the questions, to which cursory answers are given and on which no discussion is permitted, are the only opportunities by which Members may acquire information. Ministers in charge of Departments report once or twice a year what they choose of what their Departments have done.

Members of Parliament may move to reduce the amount Parliament is to vote for the Department in question, as a protest against something that displeases them, or as a matter of political form. Such motions are usually defeated or withdrawn. If, however such a motion be carried, the Government may resign, if the question involved be important. Generally, in such rare cases, the Government brings the vote up again another day, and, by rallying its supporters, it defeats the motion. Perhaps as a result of the incident the Minister whose Department has been criticised, moves on to another Department. His old place is taken by one whose policy differs but little from his own.

The House of Commons has no effective check on the doings of the Cabinet: it knows very little of what the Cabinet is actually about; the Press is given more information on questions of State than are the ordinary Members of Parliament.

The House of Lords, with its hereditary members, can check and thwart the doings of the Government more effectively than can the House of Commons, although its power is specifically limited. Its Members are not dependent on the machinery of the Party to secure their election. Their Parliamentary seats are theirs for life: no-one can dislodge them. The older Lords, at least, are probably no longer seeking the favour of Party leaders and Members of the Government to assist their personal fortunes. Though, perhaps, less open to personal corruption than the ambitious political hacks of the House of Commons, the Members of the House of Lords are, of course, even more surely lined up as one man against the emancipation of the proletariat and in defence of the present system.

In all this the electors are remote outsiders. They have no hold on the Members of the House of Commons who are supposed to represent them. They must decide for which candidate to vote on the general programme of the Party promoting the candidature, for, if returned, the Member will have no power except through his Party. No item of the Party programme is binding, no pledge given by the candidate or his

Party can be relied on. The programme is enunciated during the election in vaguely-worded speeches and manifestos, every point in which will probably be discarded. Not until the next election will the voter have another chance to pass judgement on the actions of the candidate who won the seat in his local constituency, or on those of the Government in power. The Member, meanwhile, has probably been merely a cipher in Parliament; the Government has done nothing pleasing to the elector; but the opposing Party, in the vague compound of catch-cries called its programme, offers nothing that promises satisfaction. The constituency is vast: the electors have no personal knowledge of either candidate. The election is decided by such questions as which Party machine has most systematically traced the absent voters and made the best arrangements to bring them to the poll, which Party has the most motor cars lent to it for taking voters on free rides to the polling booth, which Party is served by the local paper having the largest circulation in the district.

Even were it possible to democratise the machinery of Parliament, its inherently anti-Communist character would still remain. The King might be replaced by a President, or all trace of the office abolished. The House of Lords might disappear, or be transformed into a Senate. The Prime Minister might be chosen by a majority vote of Parliament, or elected by referendum of the people. The Cabinet might be chosen by referendum, or become an Executive Committee elected by Parliament. The doings of Parliament might be checked by referendum.

Nevertheless, Parliament would still be a non-Communist institution. Under Communism we shall have no such machinery of legislation and coercion. The business of the Soviets will be to organise the production and supply of the common services; they can have no other lasting function.

Second Version

Part One

Workers Dreadnought January 27th 1923

Under Communism all shall satisfy their material needs without stint or measure, from the common storehouse, according to their desires. Everyone will be able to have what he or she desires in food, in clothing, books, music, education and travel facilities. The abundant production now possible, and which invention will constantly facilitate, will remove any need for rationing or limiting of consumption.

Every individual, relying on the great common production, will be secure from material want and anxiety.

There will be no class distinctions. These arise from differences in material possessions, education and social status. All such differences will be swept away.

There will be neither rich nor poor. Money will no longer exist, and none will desire to hoard commodities not in use, since a fresh supply may be obtained at will. There will be no selling, because there will be no buyers, since everyone will be able to obtain everything desired without payment.

The possession of private property, beyond that which is in actual personal use, will disappear.

There will be neither masters nor servants. Because all will be economically equal — no individual will be able to become the employer of another.

Children will be educated up to adult age, and adults will be able to make free, unstinted use of all educational facilities in their abundant leisure.

Stealing, forgery, burglary, and all economic crimes will disappear, with the vast and bjectionable apparatus which at present exists for preventing, detecting, and punishing crime.

Prostitution will become extinct; it is a commercial transaction, dependent upon the economic need of the prostitute and the customer's power to pay.

Sexual union will no longer be based upon material conditions, but will be freely contracted on the basis of affection and mutual attraction. The marriage laws, having become obselete, will disappear. If people have ceased to be happy together they will part in freedom and without incurring the stigma of social disapproval.

The birth of children will cease to be prevented by reason of poverty.

Material anxiety being removed, and the race for wealth eliminated, other objects and ambitions will take the place of the individual struggle for existence and material wealth. Since all will benefit from the labour of all, praise will be given, not to the wealthy, as at present, but to those who prove skilful and zealous in the common service.

Emulation in work will take the place of emulation in wealth.

With the disappearance of the anxious struggle for existence, which saps the energy and cripples initiative, a new vigour, a new independence will develop. People will have more courage to desire freedom, greater determination to possess it. They will be more exacting as to their choice of a vocation. They will wish to work at what they enjoy, to order their lives as they desire. Work will be generally enjoyed as never before in the history of mankind.

The desire for freedom will be tempered by the sense of responsibility towards the commonweal, which will provide security for all.

Public opinion provides a stronger, more general compulsion than any penal code, and public opinion will strongly disapprove idleness and waste.

To secure the abundant production necessary to Communism, and to cope with the ever-growing complexity of modern life and requirements, large-scale production and co-operative effort is necessary. The people of today would not be willing to go back to producing everything by hand in domestic workshops; were they to do so, they could not maintain the population in comfort and with reasonable leisure. The people of today would be unwilling to abandon all the productive factories, the trains, the electric generating stations and so on. The retention of such things necessitates the working-together of large numbers of people. As soon as numbers of people are working together and supplying with their products numbers of other people, some sort of organisation of work and of distribution becomes inevitable. The work itself cannot be carried on without organisation. In each industry, either the workers concerned in the work must form and control the organisation, or they will be under the dominion of the organisers. The various industries are interlocked in interest and utility; therefore the industrial organisations must be interlocked.

When wages have disappeared, when all are upon a basis of economic equality, when to be manager, director, organiser, brings no material advantage, the desire to occupy such positions will be less widespread and less keen, and the danger of oppressive action by the management will be largely nullified. Nevertheless, management imposed on unwilling subordinates will not be tolerated; where the organiser has chosen the assistants, the assistants will be free to leave; where the assistants choose the organiser, they will be free to change him. Co-operation for the common good is necessary; but freedom, not domination, is the goal.

Since co-operative work and mutual reliance on mutual aid renders some kind of organisation necessary, the best possible form of organisation must be chosen: the test of its worth is its efficiency and the scope for freedom and initiative it allows to each of its units.

The Soviet structure of committees and delegates, built up from the base of the workshop and village assembly, presents the best form of organisation yet evolved; it arises naturally when the workers are thrown upon their own resources in the matter of government. The Soviet structure will undoubtedly be the organisational structure of Communism, at any rate, for some time to come. We live always, however, in a state of flux, and there is, and happily can be, no permanence about human institutions; there is always the possibility of something higher, as yet undiscovered.

The overthrow of Capitalism precedent to the establishment of Communism will be resisted by the possessors of wealth. Thus Capitalism will only be overthrown by revolution.

The revolution can only come when conditions are ripe for it; but opportunities may be missed: the rising may fail to take place at the opportune moment, or it may fail by mismanagement of the proletarian forces. A partial success may be achieved, and if Capitalism is not completely destroyed it may afterwards re-establish itself, as it speedily did in Hungary, as it is gradually doing in Russia.

Part Two

Workers Dreadnought February 3rd 1923

Those who are well to do under the present system are apt to oppose Communism, from conservatism and lack of imagination, and from anxiety lest the disorganisations of the transition period may destroy their present comfort. Some even fear that under Communism the emancipated workers may revenge themselves upon those who were of the employing class in Capitalist society, by degrading them to a subject position; but Communism has no place for subject classes. It has neither economic nor social distinction. It will emancipate the entire humanity.

The hard toil of the business man and his manifold anxieties are continually cited as arguments against this or that amelioration of the lot of the workers to-day. Let the exacting toil, the stupendous financial commitments, the ceaseless stupefying anxieties be admitted: Communism will remove all these. It will emancipate the business man from his business: it will free him for useful, care-free work and pleasure, from the shackles of useless toil. Nevertheless, the Capitalists of to-day have shown themselves as ready as were the feudal lords of the eighteenth century to resist the processes of evolution by force of arms and to make war to prevent the coming of the equalitarian social order.

In the contemporary cycle of civil wars, that of Finland was an early example of this fact.

The Russian Revolution of March 1917 removed the Czarist domination from Finland. Kerensky's provisional Government opposed the independence of Finland, dissolved the Finnish Parliament, which had passed a law making itself the supreme power in Finland, and ordered new elections. On one

51

occasion it posted Hussars to prevent the assembling of the dissolved Parliament, but next time only "Kerensky's seals" were on the door, and these were easily broken. Kerensky's Provisional Government lacked the strength to keep Finland within the Russian Empire. The All-Russian Workers' and Soldiers' Council, which sat simultaneously with Kerensky's Provisional Government and was steadily becoming the real power in Russia, had declared for Finnish independence. Finland at that time was considered the most democratic of countries. Its Parliament had only a single Chamber, it had a wide franchise and proportional representation, votes fort women, and women members of Parliament. In the Parliamentary elections of 1916 the Social Democratic Party had secured a majority, and a coalition had been formed. Finland had no army under the Czar: she had been policed by Russian troops, and now Finland was without an army. Finnish Capitalists had desired to retain the Russian domination and the Russian Army, but that hope had failed them. During the summer of 1917 an eight-hour working day law was enacted, and universal suffrage was extended to the field of local Government. Russia was moving towards the Bolshevist revolution, and would not interfere. There were only a few large Capitalists in Finland in the timber and paper industries, and the taking over of about ten large firms would have nationalised by industry. Already the forests belonged to the State; the Russian domination had checked the growth of powerful Finnish interests. Apparently there was nothing to prevent the country from passing on to Socialism by ordered Parliamentary stages. Yet Parliament seemed helpless. War conditions, including the British blockade, were causing a food shortage, and, though the Parliament passed a law to stop speculation in food supplies, the law failed to operate. The Coalition Government, swayed to and fro by its Social-Democratic and Capitalist members, remained inactive.

The workers were hungry: in Helsingfors, the capital, they began to seize and to distribute stocks of butter — a general strike broke out spontaneously. It lasted two days, and then was brought to an end by the efforts of the Trade Union leaders.

In October 1917 new elections were held. The Social-Democrats anticipated a clear Parliamentary majority. Instead, they lost the bare majority they had, and became a minority party. When the election figures were announced, it was found that some representatives of the bourgeois parties had obtained a greater number of votes than there were electors on the roll. Later on, when the revolution broke out, masses of voting papers made out for the Social-Democratic candidates were found locked away in the offices of presidents of electoral bureaux.

The elections had been falsified. Nevertheless, the Social-Democrats had also lost votes, because, in spite of their majority in the Coalition Government, they had been unable to safeguard the people's food and thus lost the enthusiasm of the masses.

The Coalition Government was now no more. The bourgeois groups in the Parliament voted a resolution entrusting the supreme power to a triumverate, but dared not immediately put it into practice. At the same time, they entered into negotiations with the Russian Provisional Government with a view to sharing the power and obtaining military aid to quell the people.

Then the Russian Provisional Government fell: the Russian Soviets rose to power. Lenin, who had taken refuge in Finland for a time, in returning to Russia charged the Finnish comrades to set up the Soviets; but they did not; they were opposed to revolution.

The Finnish Capitalists were now getting arms from Germany and preparing an army.

There were divided Councils amongst the Social-Democrats: some desired a general strike to secure democratic government; others did not. The various Social-Democratic factions all wished to avoid revolution. Eventually a general strike was declared. It secured a vote from the Democratic majority in the Parliament that the Parliament itself, and not merely a Government bloc, should be the supreme power in the country. This was but camouflage. The Capitalists continued preparing the army which was to attack the workers.

At the end of January 1918 the Capitalists gave the word of command for its butchers to begin the onslaught upon the workers' organisations. The Social-Democrats replied:

"The bourgeoisie is vioating and destroying democracy. To arms!"

Then, tardily, the workers took arms and met force with force. They might have been victorious; but the Capitalists procured aid from Germany. Thus Capitalism maintained its rule and revenged itself by scourging Finland with a ruthless and prolonged White Terror, in which the lives of many thousand Socialists and workers were sacrificed.

In Hungary the Liberal Minister, Count Karolyi, who had come into power through the bourgeois revolution of November 1918, surrendered his office, and called the Workers' and Soldiers' Council, the Soviets of Hungary, to take the power. He did so because Hungary had been made economically bankrupt as a result of the European War and the dismemberment to which the Allied victors had subjected her. The Soviets were soon deposed by the armed forces of foreign Capitalism.

The bloody civil strife which has taken place in Germany since the war, and the invasion of Soviet Russia by the Allied Powers, are further exampls proving that the Capitalists will fight against the introduction of Communism. Italy provides a more recent, and in some respects an even more striking example.

In Italy the Socialists were making steady progress towards a Parliamentary majority. A large number of local governing bodies already possessed Socialist majorities. The masses, through their industrial and political organisations, as well as by some local mass uprisings, were manifesting a strong desire for Socialism. In 1920 the employers in the metal industries attempted to lock out the workers. The workers were organised in the workshop committee movement, which they had formed and organised independently of the Trade Unions, without surrendering their membership of the Unions. The workshop organisations now seized the factories, protected them with barbed wire, and placed machine-guns on the roofs. Workers in other industries and on the land began to take similar action. The army was sympathetic towards the movement, the Government was powerless to intervene.

The Socialist Party and the Trade Unionists, on the other hand, were either opposed to revolution, or unprepared for it. The Communists and the Anarchists did not find themselves strong enough to take the lead. The Socialist Party decided that the affair must be left to the Trade Unions. The Trade Unions persuaded the workers to surrender the factories and to become once more obedient to the Capitalist Government and to their employers.

The Capitalists showed no gratitude for the assistance they had received from Trade Union and Socialist leaders; their main concern was to take steps to prevent the workers rising again. The great industrial Capitalists of Italy, therefore, provided the funds for Mussolini to create his Fascist Army, which attacked the Trade Union, Co-operative, Socialist, Communist and Anarchist organisations of Italy, destroying their offices and plant, breaking up their meetings, wounding, or even killing, their members and officials. The Fascisti did not stop at the Labour organisations; they resorted to violence to influence the elections, and raided the local governing bodies which had a Socialist, or even a Liberal membership, assaulting, or even murdering, the members and officials who stood for progress. Finally they took arms against the Government and established a dictatorship in Italy. In their every step the masters of the Fascisti have been the greater Capitalists of Italy, whose intention has been to prevent the emancipation of the workers and the establishment of Communism the equalitarian social order which shall establish plenty and security for all.

Many British people cling to the belief that such manifestations of militant Capitalism are unlikely to occur here. Yet there is plenty of evidence to the contrary. It is notorious that certain organisations financed by the great Capitalists have constantly employed violent rowdies to combat reform agitations. The Suffragettes, the Socialists, and the opponents of war have had to run the gauntlet of such rowdyism. The Germans, Austrians, and others suffered from it during the war-time "intern-them-all" agitation. The Curragh incident, in which officers of the British Army announced they would take sides with Ulster, in preventing the application of the Irish Home Rule Act, showed that in Britain, as elsewhere, the class in power will not stop at mere rowdyism, but will proceed to civil war in defence of its priviliges. The terrible Ulster pogroms, which were organised and approved by the rich and powerful, though carried out by hired subordinates and poor and ignorant mobs, are another proof of the fact that the British Capitalist, like any other, would be quite prepared to cast aside legality, if the law should cease to protect his priviliged position.

Part Three
Workers Dreadnought 10th February 1923

Nationalist struggles, though largely economic and bound up with the might of Empire, which assures to Big Business its control of markets, are less vital to the upholders of Capitalism, than the direct contest for the overthrow of the system itself.

When the established order is in danger its beneficiaries arm to protect it; its supporters and opponents come to blows, civil war breaks out, and, for the time being, peace is no more.

Is that as it should be? It is as it is. The inevitable must be recognised and prepared for. A determined struggle for supremacy inevitably accompanies the overthrow of Capitalism.

Experience shows that the crisis arises suddenly: the old relationship has been growing more and more strained, and suddenly the bonds are snapped and the storm bursts. We do not say that a Parliamentary crisis, could not be the last straw that would precipitate the conflict, but in none of the contemporary revolutions has this been so. We have now the recent experience of Russia, Austria, Hungary, and Italy to guide our conclusions.

Great economic pressure, and a great spiritual rebellion against the actions and ideology of those who have been in power, are the factors which produce the proletarian revolution.

Parliament must be overthrown, as part of the Capitalist system, which must be altogether destroyed, if the proletarian revolution is to succeed. There must be a clean break with the old methods of supplying the needs of the community and with the old institutions of Government; the revolution must create its own instrument.

Parliament would have to be sacrificed with the overthrow

of Capitalism, even were it conceivable that an Act of Parliament will formally declare the abolition of Capitalism. The Capitalists would resist by force the first attempt to put the Act into practice; and Parliament is not the body that could carry t.e proletarian revolution through to success in face of Capitalist revolt, which would be one of both armed and passive resistance.

The workers would be compelled to meet such a revolt with all the forces at their disposal; their most characteristic weapon is their industrial power, for the effective wielding of which they would have to be co-ordinated industrially. Every industry would be divided against itself; the owners and part of the management would take the Capitalist side; the mass of the workers the side of the working class. As in all the countries where the revolutionary crisis has appeared, the naval and military forces would be divided in the same way, though the old training and discipline might cause a larger proportion of the working-class rank and file to support the side of the master class in the Army than in industry. The final events leading up to the revolution would determine this question. If an unpopular war were the ultimate incentive to revolt, the soldiers might be the leaders of the revolution.

A little consideration of the situation arising on the outbreak of revolution, will show that Parliament and the local governing bodies, the county and borough councils, the boards of guardians, and so on, could not be the guiding and co-ordinating machinery of such a struggle; that the machinery of the struggle could take no other form than that of the Soviets.

Even in a war between rival Capitalist Governments Parliament becomes a cipher. In wartime the Cabinet more than ever ignores Parliament and assumes responsibility for conducting the war, announcing that it is "not in the public interest" for Parliament to be told much of what is going on. The Cabinet, remember, is composed of the heads of the various Departments of State, all very much controlled by the expert managers of those departments. On the military side the political and military heads of the War Office work in contact with a machine which is composed of all the officers from the highest to the lowest in the Army, and the men under their command. On the industrial side the political and technical heads of the departments work through a machine which is composed of the owners, managers and workers in all industries, factories, workshops. Great sections of industry are said to be placed under Government control, but are actually handed over to the management of the big industrial magnates. The Members of Parliament, as such, have nothing to do but make speeches. In reality they count for nothing.

The proletarian revolution is the struggle for the overthrow of the system which allows private management for private profit to monopolise the supply of the community's needs. Still more, therefore, than in the case of war between Capitalist States the struggle must assume a practical utilitarian character, and be carried out by a practical, utilitarian machinery. Since the struggle for the overthrow of Capitalism is a struggle for the emancipation of the masses from the rule of the propertied class, the officers and managers on the proletarian side will naturally be leaders chosen by their fellows. Contact with the rank and file will also naturally be by delegates and mass meetings: The services of the rank and file in the struggle will not be based upon compulsion and wagery, but on consent and enthusiasm, and a share in deciding aims and policies.

During the great world war of 1914-19, even Capitalism found that shop stewards were of use in securing output and in maintaining discipline. Though Workers' Committees were formed to protect the interests of the workers, yet in most cases, because the workers supported the war the committees increased production and greatly reduced the work of the employers' managing staff. The employers disliked and feared the Workers' Committee Movement. Yet, under the great stress of war orders, they encouraged the election of shop stewards by the women munition makers, who were largely, new-comers to industry, and were shepherded into the Unions, as a condition of their employment, by an arrangement between the engineering unions and the Government. Committees of employers and Trade Union representatives sitting outside the factories were also formed, in the effort to secure increased production, by enlisting the co-operation and goodwill of the men and women who were doing the actual work. These committees, though acting under Government auspices, had much less power to influence production than the workers' own Councils in the factories themselves.

The Workers' Committees in the factories and workshops form the basis of the Workers' Council or Soviet system, which will manage the industries under Communism.

It is sometimes contended that, though the Soviets would spring up as a necessary instrument of the struggle, should the fall of Capitalism be accompanied by civil war; yet Parliamentary Government could be reverted to, and the Soviets disbanded after the crisis were passed. Therefore, those who hold this view, and also hope that Capitalism may be abolished without a serious struggle, refuse to interest themselves in the question of Soviets.

Nevertheless, even assuming that it should be possible to pass from Capitalism to Communism without strife, the disappearance of Parliament is inevitable, whilst the complex character of modern industry, the varied needs of the people to-day, and the confusion of the transition would render the Soviets a necessary means of co-ordination, at least for some time after the overthrow of Capitalism.

Consider the situation which would arise in London, or any large city, if Capitalism were suddenly brought to an end. Consider the vast population crowded into a relatively small area, the elaborate network of tubes, trams and buses, the main-line stations, the docks, the waterworks, the gasworks, the electric generating stations, the dairies, bakeries and restaurants, the food preserving, clothing, furnishing, and other factories, the slaughter-houses, butchers', grocers' and greengrocers' and coal merchants, the markets and wholesale and retail dealers of all kinds. All these would be facing the end of the system that maintained them in their accustomed state; but millions of people would still be needing the daily supply of milk and bread to be delivered at their doors or lying ready for them at the nearest shop; they would still be needing their accustomed supply of food, fuel and means of transport. If there is a halt in the supply of the main necessities, some people at least will fail to present themselves to do their part in the daily task; the needs of masses of others may thus go unsupplied. Perhaps at the overthrow of Capitalism the workers are in the throes of a general strike, or from other causes, the wheels of industry are already dislocated, and everyone is already living a hungry, makeshift existence.

Whichever way it happens, everything has to be reorganised and built up on a new basis; a basis of production for use, not for profit. Undoubtedly a large proportion of those who used to manage the big concerns under Capitalism would refuse to fulfill such offices any more, even if asked. Undoubtedly many of them could not be trusted to occupy their old positions. Their hostility will be clearly apparant; they may already have taken to sabotage.

Meanwhile the people, the hungry millions of all sorts, will be clamouring to have their wants attended to; all with their peculiarities, their likes and dislikes, their reasonable and unreasonable prejudices; crowds of them will be ready to start looting, if they are kept waiting too long, or denied what they believe is their due.

Everyone, both as worker and consumer, has new hopes and desires, new claims upon life and the community, for has not the Workers' Revolution come? Everyone demands more clothes, more pleasure, more leisure, and more congenial employment. Only the patient people are willing to wait. Everyone, too, is demanding a new, independent status and a share in deciding how things shall be done. Many people, moreover, are finding their

61

accustomed work quite dislocated — even supposing they should be contented to continue doing it just as before.

Parliament is structurally unfitted to deal with such a situation; even a Parliament of Trade Union officials would find the difficulties insoluble. It would be compelled to appeal to the workers organised where they work. If the Soviets were not in being, it would appeal to the existing Trade Unions for assistance in establishing that essential machinery. Though Messrs. Ramsay MacDonald, J.H.Thomas and Will Thorne are Labour representatives, their position would be highly unenviable in face of such a crisis were no other machinery than that of Parliament available, should the structure of private enterprise be suddenly broken down. Imagine Mr. Thorne beseiged by the housewives of West Ham, whose supplies of food and fuel are cut off; and Mr. Ramsay MacDonald receiving wireless messages from Wales that his mining constituents are starving because the transport system is dislocated. The Labour Party members could attempt to deal with these things as representatives of their Unions, not as representatives of their constituents. Mr. Ramsay MacDonald could do nothing. He could only appeal to Mr. Thomas.

As to the borough councils, they would be only less incapable of dealing with the situation than Parliament itself. We remember the dislocations in the comparatively simple matter of war food rationing, and the groups of housewives here and there, who, through the muddling of the local Food Committee and the Ministry of Food, found themselves as "outlanders" prohibited from buying at the shops where they had hitherto dealt, and unable to procure commodities anywhere else. How should the Ministry of Food in Westminster be familiar with the shopping places of the women in Poplar? How should the Members of Parliament, or the Borough Councillors, suddenly become experts in the intricacies of a multitude of industries of which they hitherto knew nothing at all?

The only people who could deal with the great change and its new requirements are the people, all interlocked as they are, who are actually engaged in the making and transport of each product and the people who use it. The Soviets, built up according to the needs of each and all industries, would be the only solution of the new problem.

Had the factory been thrown into a turmoil of dislocation, then the workers in the factory would come together to produce order: each in the emergency would respond to the need that he should perform the task for which he had been equipped by training and for which workers were required, but some would be spared from accustomed tasks to fill the positions which had become vacant, to take stock and discover deficiencies, to acquaint absentees with the fact that work had begun again. These workers drafted to new work would be chosen for their fitness as far as could be discerned by themselves and their fellows. Each factory, each centre of work, would shoulder its own comparatively small difficulties, and thus by the co-operative effort of countless eager units the great tasks of the community, otherwise overwhelming, would be accomplished. Gradually the whole mechanism of industry would be transformed.

If the housewives had their Soviets when the great change came, they would not be found rushing frantically about the streets in search of supplies and threatening to break into the shops and storehouses because their children were hungry. If, however, they were disorganised as now, and hence terrified and distracted, it would be necessary for any who remained calm to call them together to enumerate their wants and transmit them not to a body of lawyers, journalists, and persons of all sorts at Westminster, but to the workers responsible for production, distribution and transport, in order that all might be supplied.

Part Four
Workers Dreadnought 24th February 1923

The Soviets.

The function of the Workers' Councils, or Soviets, is to administer and co-ordinate production, transport and distribution.

The functional units of the Soviets are the groups of workers of all grades, including those who are doing organising or managerial work, in the engineering, textile, or boot factory, the dockyard, the mine, the farm, the warehouse, the distributive centre, the printery, the laundry, the restaurant, and the domestic workers, whether engaged in the hotel or communal house or the individual dwellings — so long as individual dwellings continue to exist.

The Soviet Structure.

The generally accepted theoretical structure of the Soviets is as follows :

Industrial Co-ordination.

The Workshop Council, comprising all the workers in the shop.

The Factory Council, comprising delegates from the Workshop Council.

The Sub-District Council, comprising ll the delegates from the District Councils.

The District Council, comprising delegates from the Sub-

District Councils.

Inter-Industrial Organisation.

The National Council, comprising delegates from the District Councils.

Inter-Industrial Sub-District Councils, comprising delegates from the Sub-District Councils of each industry.

Inter-Industrial District Councils, comprising delegates from the Inter-Industrial District Councils.

National Inter-Industrial Council, comprising delegates from the Inter-Industrial District Councils, or in part, from the Industrial District Councils, in part from the National Industry Councils, and in part from delegates elected by sub-district mass meetings or Shop Councils.

There is thus a dual machinery :

1. For the organisation and co-ordination of each industry and service.

2. For the linking together of all industries and services.

The Soviet organisation must be tested and judged by its efficiency in supplying the needs of the people and in enabling the work itself to be healthy and enjoyable to those who take part in it.

The Workshop Councils, the councils of actual producers, must preserve complete autonomy and power of initiative, sense of responsibility and pride in the adequacy of their work. Their business and their object would be to serve the community by supplying what the people need and desire, as and when it is required.

We speak of the Workshop Councils, but under a normal state of Communism the Councils will meet only when new arrangements, plans, and ideas are to be considered and elaborated. At other times the members of the Works Council will apply themselves to their respective tasks. The managerial function will almost cease to exist in a community where all the workers in an enterprise are educated, willing co-operators in a common plan, but such managerial or directive work as may be needed will be done by those who have been chosen by their co-workers, not as a manager in the present sense, but as a leader in skill, a teacher and guide.

The Sub-District, District, and National Industrial Councils, and the various Inter-Industrial Councils, will also only meet when there are new arrangements to make, and for periodical consultation and report. Their function will be to to establish co-ordinating machinery, bureaux, telephone exchanges, as it were, between the sources of raw material and the workshops on the one hand, and the consumers of the product of the workshops on the other. The national bureaux will be responsible for import and distribution to the main supply stores of the larger areas, the sub-district bureaux will be the agencies to which the workshops will apply for their requirements.

It will not be the business of the national, district and sub-district Councils to command and direct the Workshops' Councils. The latter will be master of their craft, and fully competent to exercise it. Dictation from the so-called "higher Councils" will neither be needed, nor would it be accepted. There will be no conflict of class interest; all will be working towards a common end. The co-ordinating Councils, however — for it is as co-ordinating links that the District, Sub-District and National Councils will function — will, however, collect and distribute information amongst the districts. New discoveries will be notified to their bureaux. They will preserve technical data for reference as it may be required by any of the workshops. They will estimate and procure the supplies of raw material and finished products required.

In considering the Soviet organisation under Communism, it must always be born in mind that the social classes will have disappeared, that the economic interests of the people will be identical, and that therefore the clash of interests which keeps the members of the present legislative and administrative bodies interminably wrangling and speechifying will be no more.

Under Communism the arguments which will arise in the Soviets will be as to the efficacy of this or that technical process, as to whether this or that proposed innovation will increase or improve production — an end desired by all.

The network of committees of delegates which makes up the framework of the Soviets and links the many productive groups, and also individual producers, should not be regarded as a rigid cast-iron machinery, but as a convenient means of transacting necessary business, a practical method of organisation which gives everyone the opportunity of a voice in social management.

The various members of a community are dependent upon each other. The cotton spinning mill is operated by a number of groups of workers in the spinning mill who are dependent for the execution of their work on the cotton growers, the railwaymen, the mariners, the dockers, who provide them with the raw material of their trade. They are dependent on machine-makers, miners, electricians and others for the machinery of spinning and the power to run it, and on the weaver, the bleacher, the dyer, the printer, the garment worker and upholsterer to complete the work they have begun. In order that the spinners may do their work they are also dependent on builders, decorators, furniture makers, food producers, garment makers, and innumerable others.

The Soviets will supply an efficiency that is impossible in an industry which, on the one hand, is maintained solely from the motive of making money, competition being the only check to the supply of inferior goods and the desire to make profits a constant incentive thereto; and which, on the other hand, is carried on by wage workers, who work only to win their wages, and whose poor up-bringing, low wages, and extended hours of labour do not permit them to possess either complete health or an adequate education. The will to work, in the workers, the sense of mutuality between the producer and those for whom the goods are produced, which the Capitalist vainly seeks today in Whitley Councils, profit sharing, bonuses, and so on, will be a matter of course under Communism and the Soviets.

Part Five

Workers Dreadnought 3rd March 1923.

Those who have been students at a school of art and craft, which has been fortunate enough to be entrusted with some piece of work destined for actual use, will realise something of what industry will be under Communism. They will remember with pleasure the zealous fervour with which the students threw themselves into the effort, the friendly emulation in efficiency, the general determination to achieve as fine a result as possible in the collective work. Everyone was enthused by the thought that this was no mere exercise, but an object needed and desired. The finest and most difficult parts of the work were done by the teachers and more accomplished students, the easier and more mechanical tasks were willingly performed by those who were least advanced, who, nevertheless, felt that their turn to execute something ambitious would come with the acquisition of further skill. In the tasks set merely for their training, the students had already learnt that their own stage of progress determined the sort of exercises their teachers set them, and now when engaged in this joint enterprise, for which all had set the highest posible standard of efficiency, they realised that for the sake of the whole work no one should be allotted a part that was beyond his skill. Every student, however, even the dullest, firmly believed in his own capacity for progress — otherwise he would have given up this sort of study and turned to something else. Moreover, every student was encouraged to design, to invent, to learn, to do things that were at present beyond the range of his capacities. Every one of them spent a considerable part of his time in doing something of his own choosing, something which was to be his own creation and the expression of his own ideas. These last are the merits of the school; its demerits are that its students rarely take part in or come in contact with constructive work that is to be put to use.

The acquisition of technical efficiency is undoubtedly retarded thereby, and much of the zest necessary to the highest accomplishment is also lost.

In commercial industry the profit to the employer and the wage to the worker are placed, both by employer and by worker, before mastery of the craft and the production of useful and beautiful objects. The latter are apt to be regarded as only necessary in so far as they minister to the former. Mechanical efficiency is acquired in the practice of industry with a rapidity uncommon in the schools. Girls and boys who have worked a few months in the potteries learn to paint more accurately on slippery cups and saucers than students who have studied an equal time in the schools of art do on the paper nicely strained on their drawing-boards, using the finest sable brushes and water colours.

But the boys and girls in all but a few branches of industry soon reach the end of their progress. Their creative faculties are stultified, or altogether unawakened, because they are kept to the production of a few stereotyped objects.

Only in rare instances does commercial industry supply scope to the creative faculties. Therefore, in commercial industry there is almost no living creative art. The Wedgewood pottery is but a dead copying of a beautiful art that was once alive. The productions of the famous Copenhagen porcelain factory, though tainted by commercialism, have yet something of living and developing art in them, because the workers there are encouraged to make designs on their own account without being compelled to turn out designs continually in order to assure their living. Those workers display an interest and pleasure in their work which, in heightened measure, will obtain thoughout industry under Communism.

The craft guilds of the past were somewhat vitiated by production for profit, but they gave to their members the opportunities for enjoyable work and craft development which modern industry absolutely denies to the vast majority.

70

The Soviets under Communism will bring industry to all the best features of the school and unite them to practical work. When profit making is eliminated, the young students will be able to gain technical experience in the actual workshop without losing the opportunities for study and experiment which the school provides: the industry will have its own school departments.

To-day the opponents of Communism turn to Russia for evidence against Communism and to prove the failure of the Soviets. It cannot be stated too emphatically that the Russian Revolution has not succeeded in establishing Communism, and that the Soviet Constitution has only been very partially applied. Moreover, the Russian Soviets are not regularly constituted, since they include representatives of political parties, representatives of political groups of foreigners living in Russia, representatives of Trade Unions, Trades Councils, and Co-oprative Societies, as well as representatives of the workshops.

Pravda of April 18th, 1918, published the following regulations for the Moscow Soviet elections:—

"Regulations for Representation.
"Establishments employing 200 to 500 workers, one representative; those employing over 500, send one representative for every 500 men. Establishments employing less than 200 workers, combine for purpose of representation with other small establishments.
"Ward Soviets send two deputies, elected at a plenary session.
"Trade Unions with a membership not exceeding 2,000, send one deputy; not exceeding 5,000, two deputies; above 5,000, one for every 5,000 workers, but not more than ten deputies for any one union.
"The Moscow Trades' Council sends five deputies.
"Political parties send 30 deputies to the Soviet: the seats are allotted to the parties in proportion to their membership,

providing the parties include four representatives of industrial establishments and organised workers.
"Representatives of the following National non-Russian Socialist parties, one representative per party, are allotted seats:—
(a) "Bund" (Jewish).
(b) Polish Socialist Party (Left).
(c) Polish and Lithuanian Social Democratic Parties.
(d) Lettish Social Democratic Party.
(e) Jewish Social Democratic Party."

The intention in giving representation to these various interests was, of course, to disarm their antagonism to the Soviet power and to secure their co-operation instead; but the essential administrative character of the Soviets was thereby sacrificed. Constituted thus they must inevitably discuss political antagonisms rather than the production and distribution of social utilities and amenities.

The Russian Soviets sprang into life in the crisis of the revolution of March 1917. They had not been created beforehand in preparation for it. They had arisen in the revolution of 1905, but had died away at its fall.

The March 1917 revolution only created Soviets in a few centres. Their number grew, and was added to by the November Bolshevik revolution; but five years later the Soviet Government admitted that the network of Soviets necessary to cover Russia was not complete. Kameneff, reporting on the question to the seventh all-Russian Congress of Soviets in 1920, stated that even where Soviets existed their general assemblies were often rare, and when held, frequently only listened to a few speeches and dispersed without transacting any real business. The Soviets were never able to cope with the productive needs.

The so-called "New Economic Policy" inaugurated by the Soviet Government in 1921; a policy that is really a reversion to Capitalism, of course, inevitably struck at the root of the Soviet idea. It has robbed the Soviets of their essential function — the administration of industry — and has transformed them into political, and to a large extent powerless, bodies.

The introduction of the New Economic Policy came as the climax of a retrogressive cycle. At the height of the revolutionary wave had come the call, partially responded to, for the management of industry by the Workshop Councils: then, with the ebbing of the tide and with the growth of reactionary tendencies in the bodies possessing coercive authority, the Workshop Councils were superseded. Management boards were established, consisting of representatives of the Factory Committees, the Trade Unions, and the Council of National Economy, a body created jointly by the Trade Unions and the Soviets. Then followed management by a single person, the Workshop Councils being deprived of all right to interfere in the management of the factories, save indirectly, through their minor share in the election of officials and boards of management. Thus by reducing the functions of the Workshop Councils, the return to private ownership and management of industrial enterprises was facilitated.

The Russian Soviets do not administer production, distribution and transport. They merely elect a proportion of those who have a share in administering certain industries.

The Workshop Council, the basis upon which the Soviet structure is theoretically supposed to be built; the local soviet, often in Russia a diversely mixed body, has but little autonomy. It is dominated by the Councils of delegates from wide areas, or the representatives who are endowed with an increasing measure of coercive authority the further they are removed from the workshop.

Part Six

Workers Dreadnought 10th March 1923
(Continued from last week.)

C. Zinoviev, at the Second Congress of the Third International in Moscow, introduced a Thesis, declaring that no attempt should be made to form Soviets prior to the outbreak of the revolutionary crisis. It was argued that, as such bodies would be powerless, or nearly so, their formation might bring the conception of the Soviets into proletarian contempt. The Thesis was adopted by the Congress, without discussion, and thereby became an axiom of the Third International.

This decision was of far-reaching significance: it meant that the Third International would no longer support the formation of Workshop Councils; and the building of an organisation upon the foundation of the Workshop Councils, taking in all workers in all industries with the revolutionary purpose of taking over and managing industry. At its inception the Third International had made much of the British Shop Stewards' Movement, of wartime growth, believing it, on the strength of Government and Press denunciations, to be a genuinely revolutionary force. Now that the Third International had set its face against pre-revolutionary Soviets, it sought to damp down Workshop Council Movements in all countries. This was a logical part of the changed policy of the Third International, which has veered round from the attempt to create new industrial revolutionary organisations, to acceptance of the existing craft unions.

The question as to whether the mere borrowed term, Soviet, shall be reserved for use in the actual crisis of revolution is of small importance, though if not used previously it would probably miss being adopted as the slogan of the revolution.

The question of postponing the creation of the actual organisation till the hour of revolutionary crisis is, on the other hand, a fundamental one.

The idea expressed and insisted upon in the thesis of Zinoviev was that the Soviet must be a great mass movement, coming together in the electrical excitement of the crisis; the correctness of its structure; its actual Sovietness (to coin an adjective) being considered of secondary importance. A progressive growth, gradually branching out till the hour of crisis; a strong and well-tried organisation is not contemplated by the thesis. The need for a carefully conceived structure is ignored. Not organisation, but only propaganda for the Soviets is recommended.

Russia's dual Revolution was an affair of spontaneous outbursts, with no adequate organisation behind it. The Trade Unions, always a feeble growth, were crushed by the Czardom at the outbreak of the Great War of 1914. The Revolutionary political parties could call for a revolution; but they could not carry it through; that was accomplished by the action of the revolutionary elements in the Army and Navy, in the workshops, on the railways, and on the land. That these revolutionaries at the point of production were mainly unorganised was a disability, not an advantage. In Russia the government, first of the Czar, then of Kerensky, crumbled readily under the popular assault. The disability arising from the disorganised state of the workers was not felt in its full weightiness until after the Soviet Government had been established. Then it was realised that, though the Soviets were supposed to have taken power, the Soviet structure had yet to be created and made to function. The structure is still incomplete: it has functioned hardly at all. Administration has largely been by Government departments, working often without the active, ready co-operation, sometimes even with the hostility of groups of workers who ought to have been taking a responsible share in administration. To this cause must largely be

75

attributed Soviet Russia's defeat on the economic front.

www.ingramcontent.com/pod-product-compliance
Lightning Source LLC
Chambersburg PA
CBHW060206290526
45789CB00003B/1187